ANIMALS IN DANGER!

Orangutans

Nancy Dickmann

BROWN BEAR BOOKS

Published by Brown Bear Books Ltd
4877 N. Circulo Bujia
Tucson, AZ 85718
USA

and

Unit 1/D, Leroy House
436 Essex Rd
London N1 3QP
UK

ISBN 978-1-78121-444-2 (library bound)
ISBN 978-1-78121-466-4 (paperback)

Library of Congress Cataloging-in-Publication Data available on request

Text: Nancy Dickmann
Designer: Supriya Sahai
Design Manager: Keith Davis
Picture Researcher: Laila Torsun
Editorial Director: Lindsey Lowe
Children's Publisher: Anne O'Daly

Manufactured in the United States of America
CPSIA compliance information: Batch#AG/5623

Picture Credits

The photographs in this book are used by permission and through the courtesy of:

Front Cover: iStock: USO.
123rf: Andrey Gudkov 1, 12–13; Alamy: National Geographic Creative 10, RSMultimedia 16, Rosanne Tackaberry 16–17; Dreamstime: Derrick Neill, 8–9; iStock: CraigRJD 14–15, KvitaJan 4, robschwankhuizen 5, USO 18–19, 20; Shutterstock: clearviewstock 14, JMcurto 12, Petr Klabal 21, Sergey Oryadnikov 6–7, 8, Andrey Shcherburkhin 10–11, Richard Whitcombe 18.

All other artwork and photography © Brown Bear Books.

t-top, r-right, l-left, c-center, b-bottom

Brown Bear Books has made every attempt to contact the copyright holder. If you have any information please contact: licensing@brownbearbooks.co.uk

Websites

The website addresses in this book were valid at the time of going to press. However, it is possible that contents or addresses may change following publication of this book. No responsibility for any such changes can be accepted by the author or the publisher. Readers should be supervised when they access the Internet.

Words in **bold** appear in the Useful Words on page 23.

Contents

What Are Orangutans? 4
Habitat and Food 6
Using Tools 8
How Orangutans Communicate .. 10
Baby Orangutans 12
Orangutans in Danger 14
Helping Orangutans 16
What's Next? 18
Orangutan Helpers 20
Fact File 21
Try It! 22
Useful Words 23
Find Out More 24
Index 24

What Are Orangutans?

Orangutans are large **apes**. They are related to chimps and gorillas. They are related to humans, too!

Male orangutans are bigger than females. They often grow large **cheek pads**.

IN DANGER!

Orangutans are in danger of dying out. People need to protect them.

Orangutans have long, strong arms. Their legs are fairly short. When they walk, they put their fists on the ground.

Habitat and Food

A **habitat** is the place where an animal lives. Orangutans live in tropical **rain forests**. Their long arms help them swing through the trees. They make nests in the branches. They sleep in these nests.

Orangutans only live on two large islands in southeast Asia.

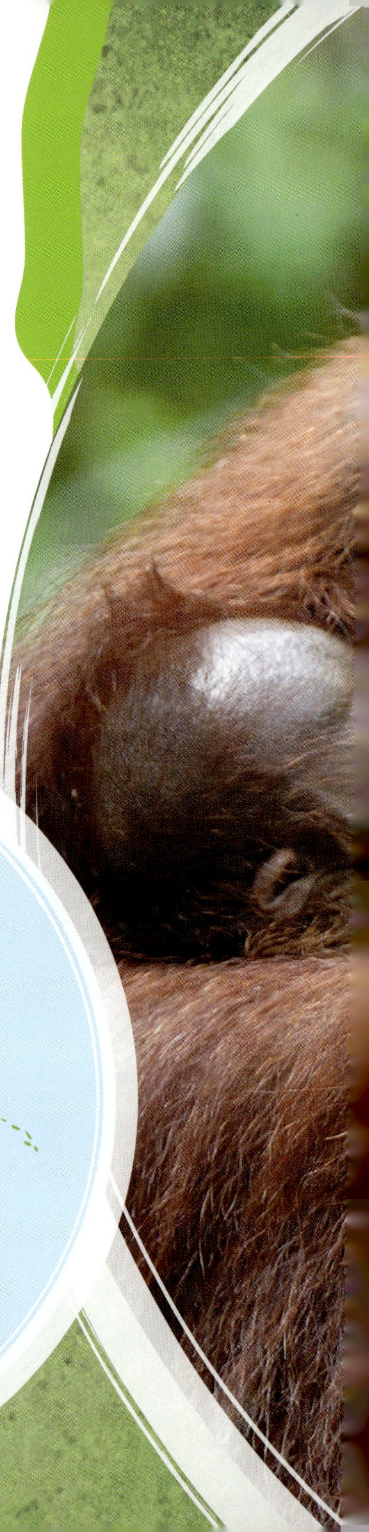

WOW!

The name "orangutan" comes from a local language. It means "person of the forest."

Orangutans mostly eat fruit. They also eat leaves, flowers, and bark. They eat insects and eggs, too.

Using Tools

Orangutans are very clever. They make simple tools. They break off a twig. They strip off the leaves and bark. Then they use the stick as a tool.

Orangutans use leaves as umbrellas.

Orangutans use their stick tools to scratch themselves. They poke them into trees to reach honey or insects. They use them to get seeds from fruit.

How Orangutans Communicate

Orangutan communicate with sounds. They call out to each other. They laugh when they play.

One kind of call is called a kiss-squeak.

Male orangutans can make loud calls. A **throat sac** makes the sound louder. The noise warns other males to stay away.

WOW!

Orangutans cup their hands to make their call lower. This might make the orangutan sound bigger.

Baby Orangutans

A baby orangutan is small. It feeds on its mother's milk. It clings to her wherever she goes. After about two years, the baby starts to explore.

A baby orangutan has white patches around its eyes.

An orangutan stays with its mother for at least six years. The mother teaches it to find food. She shows it how to make a nest and use tools.

Orangutans in Danger

Orangutans are **endangered**. Their numbers are going down. They are at risk of dying out. Tigers sometimes hunt orangutans. But the biggest threat is humans.

There are tigers on Sumatra, but not Borneo.

Poachers kill thousands of orangutans each year. They might eat their meat or sell it. Some poachers catch young orangutans. They sell them as pets.

Helping Orangutans

There are laws to protect orangutans. It is **illegal** to hurt or kill them. It is illegal to sell them. People are not allowed to keep them as pets.

Some land is set aside for orangutans. **Rangers** help keep them safe.

Poachers catch baby orangutans. Sometimes they kill their mothers. Workers rescue baby orangutans. The babies might go back to the **rain forest** when they are older.

What's Next?

Poachers kill many orangutans.
But that is not the only problem.
People cut down **rain forest** trees.
They use the land for farming.

Farmers plant crops where forests used to grow.

Orangutans need the rain forests. They need them for food. They need them for shelter. Without rain forests, orangutans will die out. People need to protect orangutans. They need to protect their **habitat**, too.

WOW!

From 1999 to 2015, 100,000 Bornean orangutans died. That is about half the population.

Orangutan Helpers

These groups help orangutans:

The International Union for Conservation of Nature (IUCN) is a group of scientists. The scientists count animals. They keep track of their numbers. They decide whether an animal is **endangered**. They say when it has gone **extinct**.

The WWF is a charity. It works to keep the **rain forests** safe.

Orangutan Foundation International (OFI) is a charity. It helps care for rescued orangutans.

Fact File

Average life span:
up to 40 years

Size: up to 5 feet
(1.5 meters) tall

Arms: up to 7 feet
(2.1 meters) outstretched

Weight: up to 180 pounds
(82 kilograms)

Diet: fruit, leaves, bark,
insects, honey, eggs

WOW!
An orangutan spends about 90 percent of its time in the trees.

Try It!

Imagine that you are a scientist. You are counting orangutans in a forest. Are their numbers going down? Make a line graph to show your results.

You will need:

- graph paper
- pencil
- ruler

Year	Number
2000	45
2005	39
2010	34
2015	25

1 Write "Date" along the bottom of the graph. Write the years on the line. They should be evenly spaced.

2 Along the side, write "Orangutan Numbers." Write in numbers from 0 to 45.

3 Use the data in the table to plot the numbers on the graph.

4 Use the ruler to connect the dots. What does the line look like?

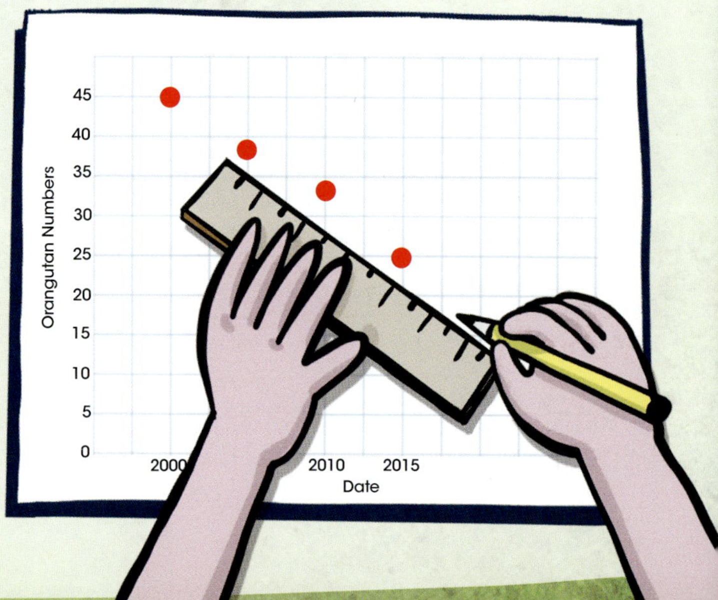

Useful Words

ape A type of animal that is closely related to humans. Humans, apes, and monkeys are in a group of animals called primates.

cheek pad A large, thick pad of flesh around the face. Only adult males grow cheek pads.

endangered In danger of dying out completely so that no more will be left.

extinct Having died out completely so that no more are left.

habitat The place where a plant or animal lives.

illegal Against the law.

poacher A person who hunts or traps animals when it is against the law.

rain forest An area in a warm part of the world where trees grow thickly.

ranger A person who works in a park or forest. Many rangers keep animals safe.

throat sac A fleshy pouch on a male orangutan's chest that makes its calls louder.

Find Out More

Websites

www.nationalgeographic.com/animals/mammals/group/orangutans/

www.orangutan.org/orangutan-facts/

www.worldwildlife.org/species/orangutan

Books

Curious About Orangutans Gina Shaw, Smithsonian, 2017

Orangutan Orphanage Suzi Eszterhas, Owlkids, 2016

Orangutans Megan Borgert-Spaniol, Bellwether Media, 2013

Index

arms 5, 6

Borneo 6, 14, 19

calls 10, 11
cheek pads 4

food 7, 9, 13, 19

habitats 6, 19

laws 16

milk 12

nests 6, 13

pets 15, 16
poachers 15, 18

rain forests 6, 17, 18, 19
rangers 16

Sumatra 6, 14

tigers 14
tools 8, 9, 13
trees 6, 9, 18

young orangutans 12, 13, 15, 17